*focus*

Meat Eaters

Plant Eaters

Dinosaurs

SIMON & SCHUSTER BOOKS FOR YOUNG READERS
An imprint of Simon & Schuster Children's Publishing Division
1230 Avenue of the Americas, New York, New York 10020

Conceived and produced by Weldon Owen Pty Ltd
61 Victoria Street, McMahons Point
Sydney, NSW 2060, Australia

Group Chief Executive Officer John Owen
President and Chief Executive Officer Terry Newell
Publisher Sheena Coupe
Creative Director Sue Burk
Concept Development John Bull, The Book Design Company
Editorial Coordinator Mike Crowton
Vice President, International Sales Stuart Laurence
Vice President, Sales and New Business Development Amy Kaneko
Vice President Sales, Asia and Latin America Dawn Low
Administrator, International Sales Kristine Ravn

Project Editor Jessica Cox
Designers Julie Brownjohn, Gabrielle Green, and Amellia O'Brick
Cover Designers Gaye Allen and Kelly Booth

Color reproduction by Chroma Graphics (Overseas) Pte Ltd
Printed by SNP Leefung Printers Ltd
Manufactured in China

A WELDON OWEN PRODUCTION

SIMON & SCHUSTER BOOKS FOR YOUNG READERS is a trademark of Simon & Schuster, Inc.
The text for this book is set in Meta and Rotis Serif.
Cataloging-in-publication data for this book is available from the Library of Congress.

ISBN-13: 978-1-4169-6466-7
ISBN-10: 1-4169-6466-5

Dinosaurs

John Long

Simon & Schuster Books for Young Readers
New York London Toronto Sydney

Contents

introducing

introducing

Rule of the Dinosaurs

Dinosaurs were a group of mostly large reptiles that dominated the living world for about 160 million years, until they suddenly disappeared about 65 million years ago (mya). They lived in a time called the Mesozoic era. Around 800 different species of dinosaurs have been identified, varying in size and shape from the ferocious predator *Tyrannosaurus* to the pigeon-size *Microraptor*. Like mammals today, these adaptable reptiles inhabited every realm of Earth, from the ocean to the skies. Today's birds are the direct descendants of predatory dinosaurs.

Evolving dinosaurs

During the 160 million years they were on Earth, dinosaurs evolved from smaller, primitive forms to larger, more specialized forms. Here we see the evolution of a lineage of predatory dinosaurs called theropods.

Herrerasaurus *This primitive theropod was about 6.5 feet (2 m) long and lived in South America during the Triassic period (220 mya).*

Feathered friend?
Since earlier relatives of *Tyrannosaurus*, such as *Dilong*, had feathers, we can predict that *Tyrannosaurus* might also have had feathers, perhaps for adornment.

Allosaurus This large hunter grew to 39 feet (12 m) long and lived in North America in the Jurassic period (150 mya).

Tyrannosaurus A massive predator that reached 46 feet (14 m) long, it lived at the end of the Cretaceous period (65 mya).

Peeling back the layers
Generally, the deeper a layer of rock, the older it is. The oldest and deepest layers contain algae. Increasingly complex plants and animals are found in the layers above. The different layers belong to different eras and periods. The Mesozoic era is divided into three main time periods: the Triassic was the oldest, the Jurassic in the middle, and the Cretaceous the most recent.

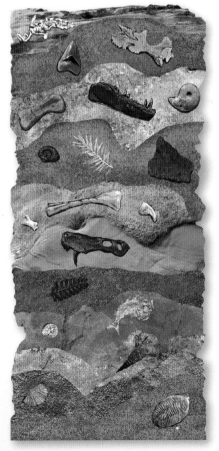

Timeline of Dinosaurs

Earth in time
Earth is around 4.5 billion years old. This span of time is divided into major blocks called eras and periods, each defined by major events.

PALEOZOIC ERA

BEFORE THE DINOSAURS

Beginning 540 million years ago (mya), the Paleozoic era is the time when life became abundant. It contains a number of periods, from the Cambrian to the Permian.

540–245 MYA

Permian:
mammal-like reptile

Carboniferous:
tree fern

Ordovician:
giant cephalopod

Silurian:
jawed fish

Cambrian:
trilobite

HUNDREDS OF MILLIONS OF YEARS

MESOZOIC ERA

TRIASSIC PERIOD

Dinosaurs appeared in the late Triassic after the climate had warmed up. As early reptiles dispersed, the first dinosaurs evolved. Simple modifications of their foot bones let them run faster, on two legs instead of four.

245–208 MYA

Melanosaurus
227–210 mya

Nothosaurus
227–210 mya

Euskelosaurus
227–210 mya

Alwalkeria
228–221 mya

Marasuchus
130 mya

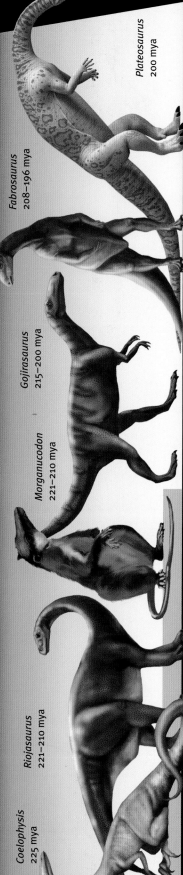

37 MILLION YEARS

Fabrosaurus
208–196 mya

Gojirasaurus
215–200 mya

Morganucodon
221–210 mya

Riojasaurus
221–210 mya

Coelophysis
225 mya

Plateosaurus
200 mya

JURASSIC PERIOD

Dinosaurs reached their peak size in the late Jurassic. As oxygen levels rose, the atmosphere became dense and humid, and plants flourished. Plant-eating dinosaurs took advantage of

Shunosaurus
169–159 mya

Dilophosaurus
202–190 mya

Scelidosaurus
202–195 mya

Dryolestes
150 mya

Limulidae

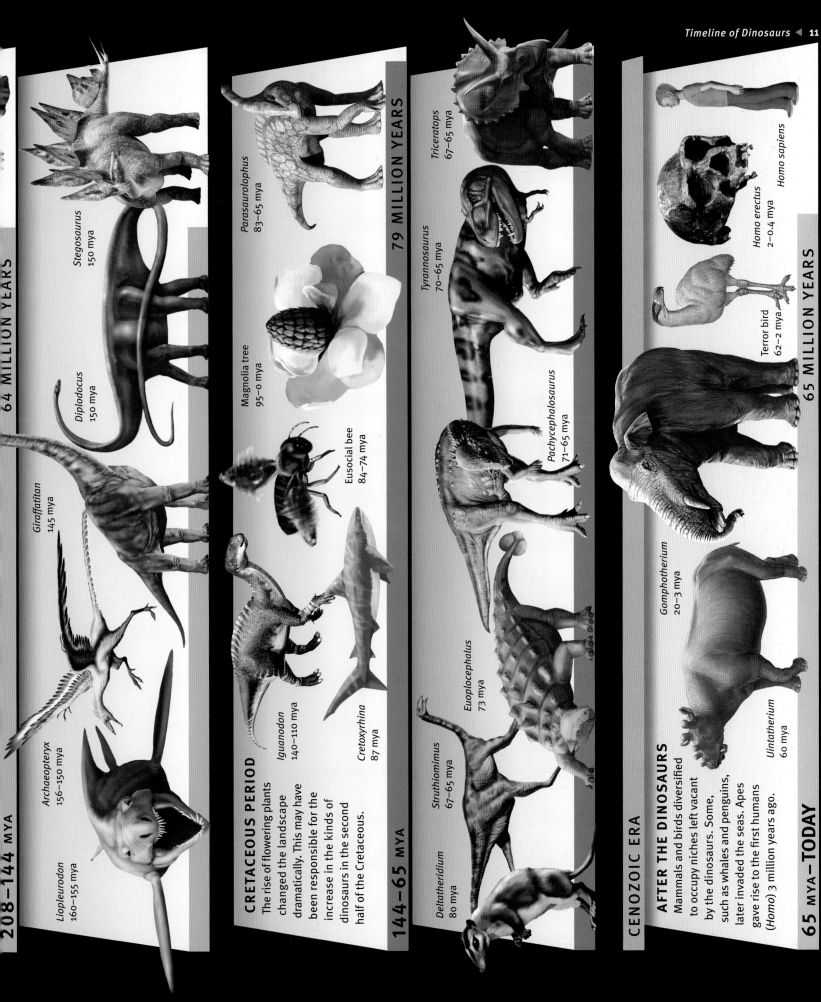

208–144 MYA

64 MILLION YEARS

Liopleurodon
160–155 mya

Archaeopteryx
156–150 mya

Stegosaurus
150 mya

Diplodocus
150 mya

Giraffatitan
145 mya

CRETACEOUS PERIOD

The rise of flowering plants changed the landscape dramatically. This may have been responsible for the increase in the kinds of dinosaurs in the second half of the Cretaceous.

Iguanodon
140–110 mya

Cretoxyrhina
87 mya

Eusocial bee
84–74 mya

Magnolia tree
95–0 mya

Parasaurolophus
83–65 mya

79 MILLION YEARS

144–65 MYA

Deltatheridium
80 mya

Struthiomimus
67–65 mya

Euoplocephalus
73 mya

Pachycephalosaurus
71–65 mya

Tyrannosaurus
70–65 mya

Triceratops
67–65 mya

CENOZOIC ERA

AFTER THE DINOSAURS

Mammals and birds diversified to occupy niches left vacant by the dinosaurs. Some, such as whales and penguins, later invaded the seas. Apes gave rise to the first humans (*Homo*) 3 million years ago.

Uintatherium
60 mya

Gomphotherium
20–3 mya

Terror bird
62–2 mya

Homo erectus
2–0.4 mya

Homo sapiens

65 MILLION YEARS

65 MYA**–TODAY**

Dinosaurs Emerge

Triassic

When the Triassic period began, about 240 million years ago, all the land on Earth was concentrated in one giant supercontinent, which we now call Pangaea. The climate was cool at first, but then warmed and became seasonal, which provided a varied landscape. This allowed the first dinosaurs, mammals, and flying pterosaurs to evolve. Pinelike trees and cycads dotted a landscape where small lizard-like reptiles lived alongside larger mammal-like reptiles and giant river-dwelling amphibians. By the close of the Triassic, arid conditions formed desert-like environments in equatorial parts of Pangaea.

Eudimorphodon *One of the first pterosaurs, Eudimorphodon had a short head with small teeth, and probably preyed on insects.*

Plateosaurus *Growing up to 33 feet (10 m) in length, the common Plateosaurus was one of the largest dinosaurs of the Triassic.*

Coelophysis *This long-necked predatory dinosaur lived in large herds. Its fossils have been found in mass grave deposits.*

The Triassic world
During the Triassic period, all of the major continents were joined as Pangaea. This supercontinent was surrounded by a superocean, known as Panthalassa.

- ▢ Triassic landmasses
- ▢ Modern coastlines
- ▢ Location of modern continents

LAURASIA
Eurasia
North America
North China
Paleo Tethys Sea
PANGAEA
Panthalassa
Arabia
South China
South America
Africa
Tethys Sea
GONDWANA
India
Australia
Ischigualasto formation
Antarctica

Dragonflies *Triassic dragonflies, similar to modern species but with 9-inch (20-cm) wingspans, were tasty meals for small, fast dinosaurs.*

Life in the Ischigualasto

In northwest Argentina, 226–220 million years ago, lived some of the earliest dinosaurs and mammals. Small predators, like the dinosaur *Eoraptor*, had to contend with larger predatory mammal-like reptiles. Other dinosaurs, such as *Plateosaurus*, ate plants.

Neocalamites *This common type of horsetail plant lived at the water's edge and grew several feet high.*

Ischigualastia *This mammal-like reptile was 6.5 feet (2 m) long and ate plants, which it cropped with its horny beak.*

Eoraptor *This predatory dinosaur was 3.3 feet (1 m) long. Its name means "dawn thief."*

Giants and Hunters
Jurassic

In the Jurassic period, the climate was warm and increasingly humid, which enabled large forests to flourish. This set the stage for the gargantuan long-necked sauropods to evolve. In turn, large predatory theropods evolved to hunt them. Other plant-eating dinosaurs developed armor to protect themselves, while pterosaurs dominated the skies above. The first crocodiles appeared, and many kinds of small, shrewlike mammals lived in the shadow of the dinosaurs. In the seas, giant marine reptiles, such as ichthyosaurs, fed on a great diversity of bony fish. It was at this time that the first bird, *Archaeopteryx*, evolved in Europe.

Apatosaurus *This sauropod reached 70 feet (21 m) in length. It may have used its huge weight to push over trees, so it could get to the newly forming leaves.*

Life in the Morrison
Some 150 million years ago, a diverse dinosaur community was thriving on a vast North American flood plain surrounded by a sparse forest of conifer trees and ferns. The largest dinosaurs, the sauropods, were hunted by theropods, while smaller dinosaurs stalked frogs, salamanders, and flying pterosaurs.

Stegosaurus *This armored plant eater reached 30 feet (9 m) in length, and protected itself with four sharp tail spikes.*

Marshosaurus *With a name meaning "Marsh's lizard," this 16-foot (5-m) predatory theropod had small forearms and sharp, curved teeth.*

Lizards and tortoises *Early lizards, tortoises, frogs, and salamanders, which closely resembled those of today, existed together in the waterways.*

North America
Morrison formation
Eurasia
LAURASIA
Panthalassa
Africa
South America
Tethys Sea
GONDWANA
Australia
Antarctica

The Jurassic world
North America drifted away from Eurasia and Africa, opening up the ancient Atlantic. In the south, the landmass Gondwana remained largely intact.

☐ Jurassic landmasses
☐ Modern coastlines
☐ Location of modern continents

Pterosaurs *Several species of small pterosaurs existed during the Jurassic. Some had long tails and others had no tail at all. They mostly fed on fish.*

Plant life *Large conifer trees, such as* Araucaria, *dotted the landscape, shedding pinecone-like nuts onto the ground.*

Goniopholis *One of the first crocodiles,* Goniopholis *lived in the rivers. It hunted water-dwelling prey, as well as creatures that came to drink.*

Taking to the Skies

Cretaceous

During the Cretaceous period, the moving continents created a more seasonally variable climate. Temperatures remained warm in the tropics but were cooler in the high latitudes. Throughout the world, dinosaurs diversified into many kinds, and birds and mammals also became more abundant. The first flowering plants—angiosperms—appeared in the early Cretaceous and gradually took over the landscape. At the end of the period, a massive meteorite impact threw the world into chaos. This may have caused the decline of the dinosaurs, although some groups had already begun to die out.

Haopterus This long-snouted pterosaur had many small teeth and a wingspan of 4 feet (1.3 m). It probably ate small fish from lakes.

Life in the Yixian

In China, 130 million years ago, many kinds of dinosaurs and early birds lived alongside a huge lake. Dinosaurs that fell into the lake's quiet waters were buried by sediment, which preserved the extraordinary details of their skin. These remains show that some dinosaurs were feathered, just like birds.

Bennettitales These seed-bearing plants were similar to cycads, with stout woody trunks and branching leaves.

Psittacosaurus This plant-eating dinosaur was 3 feet (1 m) long. It had a parrot-like head and quill-like structures on its tail for protection.

Repenomamus The skeletons of juvenile Psittacosaurus were found inside the gut of Repenomamus, which indicates they were prey and predator.

The Cretaceous world

The southern landmass of Gondwana broke into separate landmasses. Cold weather dominated the high latitudes, and polar climates existed.

- Cretaceous landmasses
- Modern coastlines
- Location of modern continents

Microraptor This small carnivorous dinosaur was about the size of a chicken, with branched feathers on both its arms and its legs.

Dilong Dilong was a 5.2-foot (1.6-m)-long, feathered tyrannosaur. Its name means "emperor dragon."

Conifers These dominant trees of the early Cretaceous gave way to flowering plants by the end of the period.

Jeholopterus This pterosaur had a wingspan of 23.5 inches (60 cm). Its sharp teeth and broad face indicate it was probably adapted to eat insects.

The beginning of the end
This killer event probably occurred at the Yucatan Peninsula of Mexico. Deep underground is a large crater, almost 125 miles (200 km) wide. Surface rocks show evidence of being tossed around by tsunamis and earthquakes.

Stage 1: the impact
The colossal impact of the meteorite strike incinerates all life within a wide radius, and ejects superheated debris from the vaporized meteorite high into the upper atmosphere.

Stage 2: tsunamis and volcanoes
The vaporized material cools, and dust remains in the atmosphere. Aftershocks cause earthquakes. On the opposite side of the planet, shockwaves from the impact cause volcanoes to erupt.

The End of the
Dinosaurs

About 65 million years ago, Earth was hit by a massive meteorite, 4 to 6 miles (7 to 10 km) in diameter. Traveling at 7 miles (11 km) per second, it punched a giant hole in Earth's atmosphere and vaporized on impact. The explosion filled the upper atmosphere with dust, which stopped sunlight from reaching plants and trapped ultraviolet rays, warming the planet. It probably weakened Earth's crust, causing immense volcanic eruptions to spew forth. The dinosaurs died out at this time, along with other giant reptiles—the pterosaurs, mosasaurs, and plesiosaurs—and some marine invertebrates such as coiled ammonites.

Other theories
Some believe the dinosaurs died out because they failed to adapt to rapid climate change. Others think the cause was volcanic gas poisoning or genetic mutations.

Cold climate change The moving continents deflect warm currents, and colder water from the poles cools the oceans, forming ice caps.

Hot climate change As greenhouse gases are emitted into the atmosphere, heat is trapped from the Sun and the planet heats up.

SURVIVORS OF THE EXTINCTION

Many reptiles and amphibians, such as turtles, crocodiles, frogs, and salamanders, survived this event. Birds and mammals also survived.

The hoatzin is a primitive South American bird with wing claws, similar to early prehistoric birds.

Stage 3: long-term changes
Dust and aerosols in the atmosphere cause acidic rain and an accelerated greenhouse effect. Many plants die as a result, as do the animals that depend on them for food.

A Dinosaur's
Anatomy

Dinosaurs were reptiles with legs that tucked under their bodies. While other animals crawled along, dinosaurs could walk upright and even run. Upright, they used less energy and could develop into active, warm-blooded animals, while other reptiles stayed slow and cold-blooded. There were two main dinosaur groups. The lizard-hipped dinosaurs, or saurischians, included meat-eating theropods and plant-eating sauropods. All other plant eaters were bird-hipped dinosaurs, or ornithischians.

Hips *Tyrannosaurus's hip bones—the ischium, ilium, and pubis—are typical of a lizard-hipped dinosaur. Powerful leg muscles attached to the ilium.*

Skull *The skull included the massive toothed jaws, plus many smaller bones that protected the small brain. The bones had holes in them to make them lighter.*

Stomach *Tyrannosaurus took big bites of food and did not chew, so it needed a large stomach to hold these chunks of food while they were being digested.*

Bones, organs, muscles, skin
Like all animals with backbones, dinosaurs had a framework of bone and muscle, with the soft organs nestling inside and a skin covering the outside. *Tyrannosaurus* evolved body features designed for hunting.

Back feet *These were mostly toe bones. They connected to the leg by metatarsal bones, tightly bunched to support its great weight, and the ankle bone.*

Intestines *This is where nutrients are extracted from the partly digested food. Meat eaters do not need intestines as long as those in plant eaters.*

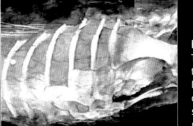

Heart of stone
This fossil shows what was once the heart of a *Thescelosaurus*. It was rich in iron, so instead of decaying after death, like most soft tissue, it turned into a mineral, and then a fossil.

Old injury
The abnormal bone growth on this *Leaellynasaura* thigh bone shows that its leg was injured—maybe by a predator or in a fall—then became infected. But it eventually healed as the dinosaur grew.

Back legs *The back legs needed to be big and powerful, to support the 5-ton (4.5-t) body as it lumbered along. But Tyrannosaurus was too big to move very fast.*

Lungs *With its big lungs acting like bellows, Tyrannosaurus could extract enough oxygen from the air to power its huge body.*

Jaws *Tyrannosaurus had an extra joint between its heavy upper and lower jaws. With this, it could open its mouth 4 feet (1.2 m) wide to take extra-big bites with its dagger-sharp teeth.*

Tail *Held up in the air, it acted like a counterbalance to all the weight at the front: it stopped Tyrannosaurus from falling over headfirst.*

Back *The back was ridged where the bones of the spine stuck up and attached to the neck and back muscles.*

Eyes *This specialized hunter's eyes faced straight ahead. Its stereoscopic, or 3-D, vision let it see all around. Small bones jutted out above the eyes.*

Body *This was shaped like a barrel to hold the huge internal organs. The lungs and heart were protected by the back ribs, while extra front ribs guarded the stomach and intestines.*

Front legs *The front legs were not much longer than a man's forearm, which is very small for such a huge animal. Tyrannosaurus did not use them at all.*

Ischium

Ilium

Pubis

Ischium

Ilium

Pubis

Two kinds of hips

The two main dinosaur groups were the saurischians, with lizard-shaped hips, and the ornithischians, with birdlike hips. Birds evolved from lizard-hipped dinosaurs to have birdlike hips.

Bird-hipped dinosaur
The long pubis bone usually faced backward, lying close to the large ischium.

Lizard-hipped dinosaur
The pubis bone usually pointed forward to form a triangle with the ilium and the shorter ischium.

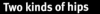

Attack and Defense
Survival

Dinosaurs had a daily battle to survive, either by defending themselves or by going on the attack. Predatory meat eaters mostly attacked using their powerful jaws full of knifelike teeth. Some had sharp claws on their feet and hands to kick and slash at exposed stomachs. They probably stalked or ran down prey, just like lions and cheetahs do today. Plant-eating dinosaurs evolved many features and strategies to defend themselves from such attacks. Some had elaborate horned frills or thick-boned heads. Others had armored plates or sharp spikes protecting their backs, or tail clubs of bone to swing at an attacker's shins.

DEFENSE OR DISPLAY?

Horned dinosaurs, such as *Protoceratops*, may have used their bony frill and horns much like modern deer use their antlers. They may have been used as a defense against attackers, or when battling other male *Protoceratops* to win a mate. Or maybe they were for display—the bigger and brighter the frill and horns, the more likely the dinosaur would be to attract a mate.

Standoff

An *Albertosaurus* lunges at a *Styracosaurus* with its powerful jaws and sharp, serrated teeth. But the horned dinosaur stands firm, its bony frill sending a warning. If really threatened, it will charge.

On the attack

For the defense

Utahraptor
Its teeth were serrated on one side. Its hands and feet ended in sickle-shaped claws.

Deinonychus
It may have hunted in packs, combining speed with its teeth and sickle-shaped claws.

Iguanodon
It lived in herds to intimidate attackers. It had a sharp thumb spike on each hand.

Allosaurus
It had sharp teeth, strong claws, and small horns above its eyes.

Troodon
Its large brain helped it hunt. It had eyes that faced partly forward to see prey better.

Baryonyx
Its hooked hand claws speared fish. Its long, crocodile-like jaws finished them off.

Ankylosaurus
It had thick, bony armor that included spikes along the back and a powerful tail club.

Stegoceras
It had a thick, domed skull with encircling spikes, good for ramming.

Diplodocus
Its massive body weight was aided by long hand claws and a tail it could crack like a whip.

Dinosaurs and
Flight

Small predatory dinosaurs started to grow feathers at least 150 million years ago. At first, simple feathers covered the body, perhaps for warmth. Then they became bigger and more elaborate, and were perhaps used to attract a mate. The arm and finger bones became more like wings, allowing some theropods to glide from tree to tree. But no feathered dinosaur could truly fly. The first birds, such as *Archaeopteryx*, could. They had long arms with wings and a tail full of flight feathers, but their skeleton was similar to that of theropods such as *Velociraptor*. Paleontologists now agree: these first birds evolved from dinosaurs.

FROM ARM TO WING

To evolve from a dinosaur's arm to a bird's wing, the wrist changed, the bones got longer and lighter, and the feathers appeared and then got larger. These changes allowed the dinosaurs to take off from the ground and remain airborne.

Sinosauropteryx Short feathers covered its body. The bones of its arms were short, like most theropods.

Caudipteryx Larger, detailed feathers adorned its arms and tail, and the finger bones were longer.

Dilong *This early Chinese cousin of* Tyrannosaurus *was 5.5 feet (1.6 m) long. Its feathers were longer and more developed than those of* Sinosauropteryx.

Velociraptor *This dinosaur from China had a small bone in its wrist that birds also have, as well as a wishbone. Its arms and fingers were the same length as the wings of early birds.*

Caudipteryx *This turkey-size dinosaur from China was the first nonflying dinosaur to develop large, elaborate feathers on its arms, perhaps for display.*

Sinosauropteryx *Found in China, this was the first known feathered dinosaur. It was entirely covered with short, hairlike feathers. But its arms were too short for flight.*

Unenlagia *This South American dinosaur had a special ability—it could fold and even flap its arms the way birds do. But it was too big to fly.*

The race to fly

Paleontologists have recently found several feathered dinosaurs in China that date from about 130 million years ago. These feathered fossils have completely changed our ideas about the origins of birds. They clearly show that small, feathered, meat-eating dinosaurs evolved into true flying birds.

Microraptor It had well-developed feathers. The longer arm and finger bones were more hollow, making them lighter.

Archaeopteryx Longer, lighter arm bones with complex wing feathers, plus a fan of tail feathers, allowed true flight.

Archaeopteryx *This was the first bird. About the size of a crow, its skeleton was like* Microraptor's, *but specialized flight feathers on its arms let it truly fly.*

Microraptor *This pigeon-size dinosaur had well-developed feathers on its arms and also on its legs. It could probably glide from tree to tree, catching insects.*

Thief with four wings
This fossil of *Microraptor*, which means "little thief," shows how its feathers formed "wings" on both its arms and its legs. It comes from the Liaoning fossil beds in China.

Troodon *The skeleton was like that of early birds, but its most birdlike feature was its big brain. That allowed it to process lots of information, essential when flying.*

Raising Dinosaur
Young

After dinosaurs mated, the females laid eggs—just like other reptiles and birds—then they cared for their eggs and young. Plant eaters such as *Maiasaura* nested in large groups. Some long-necked sauropods created mass nesting grounds, randomly depositing many eggs in each nest. *Oviraptor* made its nest alone, laying a neat circle of eggs. Some plant eaters cared for their newly hatched young for weeks until they could walk. During that time, the hatchlings depended entirely upon their parents for food and protection from predators. Small meat-eating dinosaurs grew more quickly, and perhaps could even run soon after hatching.

The good mother

Maiasaura means "good mother lizard." Large herds of these dinosaurs built their nests close together. They tended to their young in the nest for six to eight weeks, while the hatchlings' leg bones slowly hardened and grew strong enough for them to walk.

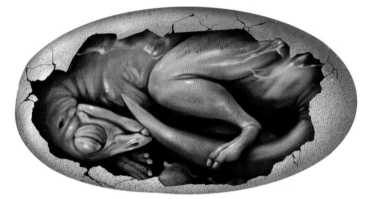

Unhatched young
The *Maiasaura* embryo has different proportions from an adult—a longer body, a shorter head and tail, and limbs that are more slender. Its bones are mostly soft cartilage.

MISTAKEN IDENTITY

The small predator *Oviraptor* got its name, which means "egg thief," because its fossil remains were first found near eggs thought to be *Protoceratops* eggs. But more recent finds show that they were *Oviraptor* eggs. It was looking after the eggs, not stealing them. One fossil was found sitting on its nest, with its front legs wrapped around its eggs to keep them warm.

Oviraptor keeping its eggs warm.

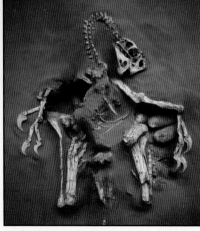

Fossilized *Oviraptor* sitting on its nest.

Different dinosaur eggs
Eggs came in many shapes and sizes. They were laid in clutches of from 7 to 50 eggs. The delicate eggs were easily trampled or cracked, so many did not survive to hatch.

Chicken
This chicken egg shows the relative size of the different dinosaur eggs.

Velociraptor
Its long, thin eggs had a pointy end, with many short ridges on the outer shell.

Hypselosaurus
This dinosaur laid oval-shaped eggs as big as footballs.

Protoceratops
This horned plant eater had long, thin eggs with wartlike bumps on the outer shell.

Sauropod
It had large, oval-shaped eggs with small bumps and short ridges on the outer shell.

Food delivery
*The parents forage
for ferns and conifer leaves.
They partly digest this food,
then feed it to their young,
whose jaws and digestive
systems cannot manage
this for themselves yet.*

Nest building *The nest is made
of piled sand with a lining of
leaves. This acts as insulation,
keeping the temperature
constant so the eggs will hatch.*

Feeding time *Young hatchlings strain
to get food from their parents. It will
be weeks before they can leave the
nest to feed, with their protective
parents close by their side.*

How eggs hatch *To hatch
out, a baby knocks against
the shell with its snout
until the shell cracks
and pieces break away.
The new hatchling is
completely helpless.*

Record-breaking
Dinosaurs

During the 160 million years that dinosaurs dominated life on Earth, they included the biggest, heaviest, and longest land animals that have ever lived. *Seismosaurus* stretched the length of 10 cars and towered as tall as a five-story building. The ground must have shook when it walked. This giant was related, however, to little chicken-size dinosaurs, which scurried through vegetation looking for seeds or insects. The smallest plant eater, *Micropachycephalosaurus*, also bears the longest name. The shortest dinosaur name is *Minmi*.

Fierce claws
Therizinosaurus snared its prey with the longest claws of all time. The terrifying claws on the back feet of *Deinonychus* were no bigger than those of a modern harpy eagle.

Modern harpy eagle
Claws 5 inches (13 cm) long

Therizinosaurus
Claws 36 inches (91 cm) long

Deinonychus
Claws 5 inches (13 cm) long

Modern basset hound
4 feet (1.2 m) long and 2 feet (0.6 m) tall

Velociraptor
6 feet (1.8 m) long and 2 feet (0.6 m) tall

An average dinosaur
Although dinosaurs are known for their incredible size, the vast majority of species were nowhere near as big as *Seismosaurus* or *Giganotosaurus*. Most were relatively small, like *Velociraptor*, a dinosaur that grew to about the size of a basset hound.

Big and small
The largest meat-eating dinosaur known from a complete skeleton is *Giganotosaurus*, but even it was dwarfed by the plant-eating sauropods. The longest dinosaur that ever lived was probably the sauropod *Seismosaurus*. Most dinosaurs were much smaller, however. The smallest dinosaur of all was *Microraptor*.

Modern boy
4.5 feet (1.4 m) tall

Modern giraffe
18 feet (5.5 m) tall

Weighing them up

The heaviest land animal alive today is the African elephant. It would have matched *Tyrannosaurus* in weight and far outweighed many smaller dinosaurs, such as *Protoceratops*. Even so, an elephant is only a fraction as heavy as *Argentinosaurus* and other giant plant-eating dinosaurs.

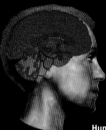

15 *Protoceratops* = 1 African elephant
880 pounds   6.5 tons (6 t)
(400 kg) each

1 *Tyrannosaurus* = 1 African elephant
6.5 tons (6 t)   6.5 tons (6 t)

1 *Argentinosaurus* = 17 African elephants
110.5 tons (100 t)   6.5 tons (6 t) each

Brainy beast

Velociraptor was one of the smartest dinosaurs. It was much smarter than a crocodile but less intelligent than any bird or mammal.

Human The most intelligent species known to exist

Velociraptor Smarter than almost all dinosaurs, except for *Troodon*

Stegosaurus One of the least smart of all dinosaurs, a dull-witted plant eater

PLANT EATERS AND MEAT EATERS

As in any food chain, many more dinosaurs ate plants than ate meat. Of dinosaur fossils found, about 65 percent are plant eaters. If we could count the individual dinosaurs that lived, the proportion of plant eaters would be even greater.

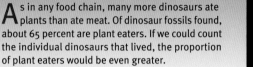

Plant-eating dinosaurs 65%   Meat eaters 35%

Longest dinosaur
Seismosaurus
150 feet (45 m) long and
18 feet (5.5 m) tall at shoulder

Smallest dinosaur
Microraptor
30 inches (76 cm) long and
10.5 inches (25 cm) tall

Largest meat eater
Giganotosaurus
47 feet (14 m) long and
12 feet (3.6 m) tall at shoulder

BRAIN POWER

A dinosaur's intelligence can be estimated by comparing the size of its brain to its body size. This gives us their EQ (or encephalization quotient). The smartest dinosaurs were small, fast-moving meat eaters from the late Cretaceous period, such as *Troodon*. They were about as smart as a modern ostrich and much smarter than a crocodile. Plant-eating dinosaurs could survive with relatively smaller brains.

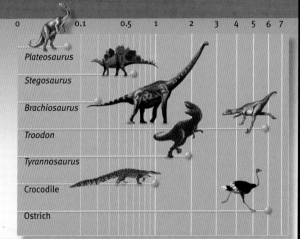

	0	0.1	0.5	1	2	3	4	5	6	7
Plateosaurus										
Stegosaurus										
Brachiosaurus										
Troodon										
Tyrannosaurus										
Crocodile										
Ostrich										

From Bone to Stone
Fossils

Fossils tell us everything we know about dinosaurs. Unfortunately, however, dinosaur fossils are rare. To become a fossil, a dead dinosaur had to be buried quickly, before it decayed to nothing or was eaten by a scavenger. If a dinosaur died in or near a river, lake, or shallow sea, its body might have been covered quickly by silt and sand. But usually the flesh decayed, and only the hard bones and teeth became fossils. Occasionally, a flood, mudslide, or ash buried a dinosaur. Then the fossils might include impressions of feathers and skin. Very rarely, bacteria preserved internal organs. Sometimes, dinosaur footprints—called trackways—and dung turned into fossils.

Battle to the death
While a *Velociraptor* was fighting with a *Protoceratops* about 70 million years ago in Mongolia, a wall of wet sand from a huge sand dune suddenly collapsed on them, instantly killing and burying the dinosaurs.

Other kinds of fossils
This 380-million-year-old fish skull was preserved after the bones were rapidly encased in limestone shortly after the fish died. Later, scientists dissolved the limestone with acid, revealing the perfectly preserved 3-D fossil.

70 million years ago *A huge, wet sand dune collapses on the battling dinosaurs. Entombed under layers of sand, their flesh and organs rot, but their skeletons, still locked together, are preserved.*

Another theory
It is also possible that each dinosaur died separately and became mummified, or dried out. The next flood washed the two mummies together, hooking the claw of *Velociraptor* deep inside the rib cage of *Protoceratops*.

40 million years ago
The bones compress deep down under layers of rock, while early mammals graze above. Chemicals in the groundwater convert the bones to minerals, which form rock-hard fossils.

20,000 years ago *Movements in Earth's crust and an Ice Age on the surface create new mountains. The rock layers containing the fossils are thrust toward the surface, where mammoths dwell.*

Today *Wind and water have eroded the surface rocks, exposing the fossils at ground level. Now begins the slow, careful process of freeing the fossils from the rock.*

Reading the Clues

Dinosaurs are studied from many pieces of fossil evidence. Their bones, to which muscles were attached, show us what they looked like and how their joints and jaws worked. Their fossil trackways tell us how fast they ran, and how some lived in herds. Fossil skin reveals that some dinosaurs had armored plates, some had feathers, and others had reptile-like skin. Nests and eggs provide clues as to how dinosaurs raised their young. Other fossils preserved with dinosaurs, such as plants, help us to reconstruct the environment in which they lived.

Fleshy fins *The back was covered by a fleshy frill of thin plates, supported on the spines of the backbone.*

Fossil feces
Coprolites are fossilized feces. The remains of plants or animals inside the coprolite show what the animal ate.

A fossil original
Leonardo was discovered in July 2000 by an amateur fossil hunter near Malta, in Montana, USA. The next summer, a slab of rock containing the fossil was carefully cut free and taken away for study.

Muscle mass *The preserved muscles and articulated bones let us see how the limbs may have worked.*

This is a bonemap drawing of Leonardo. These illustrations are used in the scientific description of fossil finds.

Fossil footprints
Fossilized footprints tell us the rough size and weight of a dinosaur, and how it walked. The distance between steps indicates if it walked or ran, and how fast.

① **Step** Dinosaur places its foot onto soft ground.

② **Tread** Foot sinks down into the ground.

③ **Liftoff** Foot pulls out, leaving an impression behind.

Footprint As the soft ground hardens, the impression may turn to stone.

Muscles *Shoulder muscles cast in rock show us the size of the muscles and how they attached to the bone.*

Re-creating Leonardo

Leonardo the *Brachylophosaurus* is a mummified dinosaur. About 90 percent of his skeleton is covered in fossilized soft tissue, including skin impressions, casts of muscles, a tongue, internal organs, and footpads. Fossilized plants found inside his stomach reveal his last meal.

Tongue *A tongue appears to be preserved as a cast in the rock.*

Crop *The throat had a crop, like that of modern birds. This let it store and chew large amounts of plant food.*

Stomach contents *Leonardo's last meal consisted of ferns, pines, and magnolia plants. Scientists have also identified pollen from 40 different plants.*

Internal organs *The stomach and possibly the heart appear to be preserved as casts in the rock.*

BUILDING UP THE BONES

Scientists use modern technology to help them accurately reconstruct dinosaurs. They also use X-ray machines and CT-scanners to build 3-D images of what is inside a fossil without having to damage it.

Moving joints The ends of bones have cartilage pads on which they move, so as not to grind on each other. Fossilized cartilage is rare, but it is taken into account when arranging bones.

Attaching muscles Ridges and grooves in the bones indicate where muscles were attached. This is how they can be placed exactly on the skeleton.

Re-created muscles All animals have similar muscle structures. Dinosaur muscles are restored by looking at the bones, as well as the patterns in modern reptiles and birds.

Dinosaur
Hunters

Paleontologists study fossils in order to reconstruct past life and environments on Earth. They search for fossils in the field, dig them up, prepare them, and study them using microscopes, X-rays, and other techniques. Their job is not only to write reports about the significance of fossils, but also to assist with museum displays, or provide information for documentary films and books about the past. To find fossils, paleontologists study geological maps of certain regions. They focus on particular areas that have the right kinds of rocks to preserve fossils. They then mount a field expedition to go and find them.

Replica bones *Dinosaur bones are replicated by making a cast of them in silicon rubber to use as a mold. This is filled with plastic resin or fiberglass. Replica bones are lighter and can be drilled into for mounting.*

Hanging bones *As dinosaurs are often large, the skeleton needs support from above to suspend it in position. Wire struts are often used to support the skeleton from the roof.*

A CHANGING VIEW

The first dinosaur to be discovered was *Iguanodon*. How its bones have been interpreted since 1822 shows how our ideas about dinosaurs have changed with time.

Iguana Scientists first restored *Iguanodon* like a giant iguana, because its teeth resemble those of a living iguana.

Dragon In one late 1880s restoration, *Iguanodon* was made to look like a mythical dragon.

Reptile The most common restoration of *Iguanodon* during the 1900s followed a reptile model, with the tail dragging on the ground.

Iguanodon The modern reconstruction, based on the study of its skeleton, muscles, and ligaments, shows *Iguanodon* on all fours with its tail held high.

Close copy

Most dinosaur skeletons mounted for display in museums are made of replica bones so that the original fossils can be closely studied and safely locked away. However, a few museums have real skeleton mounts. Any missing bones can be replaced with those from closely related dinosaurs.

Fitting wire frame *To support the skeleton off the ground, strong metal frames hold the weight of the largest bones, or replicas. They also support the backbones.*

Welding the model *To create a lifelike posture, the metal parts of the frame that support the skeleton often have to be welded in position once the bones are held in place.*

From the field to the museum

Bones are carefully excavated, then encased in plaster jackets to keep them together. This also protects them from damage on their journey back to the museum.

Removing plaster The plaster jacket is removed and the bones are carefully cleaned up, using small electric drills and brushes.

Articulating bones The bones are laid out according to where they are found in the skeleton. Damaged bones are hardened with glues, or patched with plastic resin.

Piecing together *Using the anatomy of living reptiles and birds as a guide, the dinosaur bones are carefully fitted together. The degree of possible movement between bones also helps to determine the best posture.*

Locator map These maps show you exactly where the featured dinosaur is located. Look for the red dots on each map.

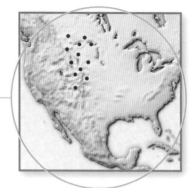

TRICERATOPS: THE FACTS

PRONUNCIATION: Try-sar-rah-tops

MEANING: Three-horned face

DATE: Late Cretaceous

GROUP: Ornithischians

DIET: Plants

SIZE: 29.5 feet (9 m) long; 10 feet (3 m) high

WEIGHT: 6 tons (5.4 t)

DISCOVERED: 1888 by John Bell Hatcher

FOSSIL LOCATIONS: Western USA and Canada

Fast facts Fast facts at your fingertips give you essential information about each dinosaur.

Time bar This time bar shows when each dinosaur lived. The bar stretches from the Triassic to the Cretaceous.

TRIASSIC

245 mya

208 mya

JURASSIC

150 mya

144 mya

CRETACEOUS

65 mya

ALLOSAURUS: THE FACTS

PRONUNCIATION:	Al-oh-saw-rus
MEANING:	Other lizard; strange lizard
DATE:	Late Jurassic
GROUP:	Theropods
DIET:	Carnivorous
SIZE:	40 feet (12 m) long, 10 feet (3 m) high
WEIGHT:	1.1–1.9 tons (1–1.7 t)
DISCOVERED:	1869 by Dr. Ferdinand Hayden
FOSSIL LOCATIONS:	Western USA

Tail *The long tail was an effective counterbalance to the front of the dinosaur.*

Allosaurus the Nightmare

Dragon

Allosaurus was the largest and one of the most common flesh-eating dinosaurs in North America during the late Jurassic. Many special features made it an effective predator: lightweight skull bones; large, curved teeth with serrations on both sides; and powerful arms and legs. It lived alongside giant sauropods like *Diplodocus*, on which it probably fed. To bring down such large animals, small groups of *Allosaurus* probably hunted together. Large males may have used the small horns above their eyes in mating battles. Some early fossils were named *Antrodemus*, meaning "nightmare dragon." This name is now no longer used.

Jaws of death
The lower jaw of *Allosaurus* had a flexible joint midway along its length. This enabled the jaws to bend outward, enlarging the mouth for a more deadly bite.

Back legs *The powerful back legs may have let Allosaurus leap onto the backs of prey and attack their spines.*

Holes for blood vessels

Jaw hinge

Middle joint to flex jaw

Flattened, serrated teeth

Size comparison
Allosaurus was three times higher than a 10-year-old, and about nine times as long.

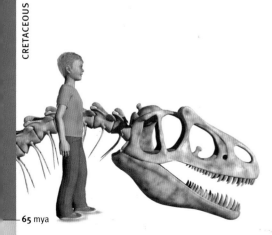

Wolves of the Jurassic
Allosaurus roamed the forests of North America 150 million years ago. Although a capable solitary hunter of small plant-eating species, *Allosaurus* also hunted in packs for giants such as *Diplodocus*. The pack would have had to inflict many wounds with teeth and claws to bring down the enormous prey.

Good head for bites
The huge skull with lightweight bones let it swiftly open its large mouth and inflict deadly bites.

Danger zone
The jaws were flexible and lined with teeth. These sawed through flesh when Allosaurus attacked its prey.

Slashers *Its muscular arms grasped on to prey while it slashed with its deadly teeth and claws.*

Camptosaurus *This was a large plant eater of the late Jurassic. It was quite possibly the favorite food of Allosaurus.*

245 mya

TRIASSIC

208 mya

JURASSIC

156 mya

150 mya

144 mya

CRETACEOUS

65 mya

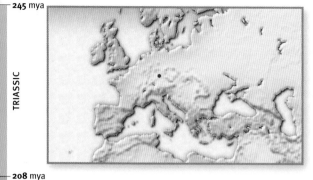

ARCHAEOPTERYX: THE FACTS

PRONUNCIATION: Ark-ee-op-ter-rix

MEANING: Ancient wing (after its light bones)

DATE: Late Jurassic

GROUP: Theropods

DIET: Carnivorous (probably insects, fish)

SIZE: 2 feet (60 cm) long; 8 inches (20 cm) high

WEIGHT: 7 ounces (200 g)

DISCOVERED: 1861 by quarry workers in Germany

FOSSIL LOCATIONS: Southern Germany

Bird brain *The birdlike brain of* Archaeopteryx *was larger than that of other theropods. This helped it process information from its senses during flight.*

Archaeopteryx and the
Ancient Wing

Archaeopteryx has long been hailed as the first bird. Its fossil remains show its wings had feathers, but its skeleton shows that it was no different from other small theropods, such as *Velociraptor*. It had a birdlike head with a narrow-toothed beak and large eye sockets and braincase. Its light and hollow bones were also birdlike. Complex feathers on its arms and tail were similar to those modern birds use to fly. Its wings were formed by arms with outstretched finger bones, and it had a long reptilian tail. *Archaeopteryx* lived near a shallow sea and may have hunted insects and small fish.

Size comparison
Archaeopteryx was slightly larger but much longer than a pigeon—much smaller than a 10-year-old.

Ground assault
Archaeopteryx probably spent most of its life on the ground, hunting insects.

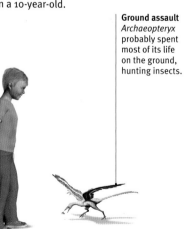

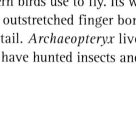

Claws on three unfused fingers in the hand

Wishbone in chest

Breastbone without a keel

Opposable (grasping) claw

Flight feathers on wing and tail

Teeth in jaws

Hip with rear-facing pubis

Tail with many bones

Feathered fossil
The fossil skeleton of *Archaeopteryx* shows feather impressions attached to the wings and tail. While it looks like a bird, other features of the skeleton are clearly those of a dinosaur.

On the nest *Like other dinosaurs, Archaeopteryx probably made a nest to protect its eggs, building it high in the treetops.*

Feathers and flight

Archaeopteryx lived mostly on the ground. It flew occasionally, running while flapping its wings to gain enough speed for liftoff. It probably lacked strength for long flights, preferring to glide.

Tree climbing
Archaeopteryx *could have used its wing claws to help it climb trees, then leap from high up into a gliding flight.*

Fluttering flight
Archaeopteryx *may have flown in short bursts by flapping its feathered wings in pursuit of insects.*

245 mya
TRIASSIC
208 mya
JURASSIC
144 mya
CRETACEOUS
70 mya
65 mya

TYRANNOSAURUS: THE FACTS

PRONUNCIATION:	Tie-ran-oh-saw-rus
MEANING:	Tyrant lizard (species name *rex* means "king")
DATE:	Late Cretaceous
GROUP:	Theropods
DIET:	Meat
SIZE:	42.6 feet (13 m) long, 16.4 feet (5 m) high
WEIGHT:	5.5 tons (5 t)
DISCOVERED:	1905 by Henry Osborn
FOSSIL LOCATIONS:	Northern USA and southern Canada

Scavenging king

Tyrannosaurus could have survived either by scavenging or by actively hunting prey. Here it feasts on the carcass of a dead *Edmontosaurus* while warding off a pack of *Troodon*.

Tyrannosaurus the
Tyrant King

Reaching 42.6 feet (13 m) in length, *Tyrannosaurus* was for many years the largest known meat-eating dinosaur. It had eyes with keen vision, strong jaws with deadly teeth serrated like steak knives, and powerful legs with sharp claws. Its arms were puny, with two-fingered hands. *Tyrannosaurus* was probably capable of hunting prey, such as big hadrosaurs. It may also have been a scavenger, using its keen sense of smell to sniff out carrion. Bone studies reveal *Tyrannosaurus* could run at about 10.5 miles per hour (17 km/h), fast enough to ambush passing prey, or to attack slower-moving herds of horned *Triceratops*.

TEENAGE GROWTH SPURT

Tyrannosaurus had a growth spurt as a teenager (14–18 years). It reached its maximum size at around 20 years, and lived to about 30 years.

5 years	10 years	15 years	20 years
Under 220 pounds (100 kg)	About 660 pounds (300 kg)	About 2.2 tons (2 t)	About 5.5 tons (5 t)

Bone-crunching jaws
Tyrannosaurus had massively powerful jaw muscles that helped it crunch up the bones of its prey. Minute shards of bone have been found in its coprolites (fossil feces).

Powerful jaw muscles

Replacement teeth growing through jaw

Size comparison
The largest skull found is 4.5 feet (1.4 m) in length, as long as a 10-year-old is tall.

Serrated teeth for cutting

Openings in skull for jaw muscles

Eyes *Forward-facing eyes gave it stereoscopic vision. This useful trait let it accurately judge the distance from its prey.*

Nostrils *The nostrils were large with special bones inside them. This restricted the body's loss of moisture after running.*

Teeth *The stout teeth had sharp ridges broken into many tiny serrations to cut easily through flesh. Powerful jaws helped crush the bones of prey.*

Two-fingered hands *The small and weak arms had only two fingers on each hand, and may not have been functional.*

Back leg *The back legs were powerful, but not strong enough for fast running without risk of major injury if it fell.*

Troodon *This 10-foot (3-m)- long theropod had a relatively large brain. It probably hunted or scavenged in packs.*

Edmontosaurus *This was a large plant-eating hadrosaur. It probably lived in herds to defend itself from attackers.*

245 mya

TRIASSIC

208 mya

JURASSIC

144 mya

CRETACEOUS

67 mya

65 mya

STRUTHIOMIMUS: THE FACTS

PRONUNCIATION: Stroo-thee-oh-my-mus

MEANING: Ostrich mimic

DATE: Late Cretaceous

GROUP: Theropods

DIET: Omnivore (small prey, insects, plants)

SIZE: 13 feet (4 m) long, 6.5 feet (2 m) high

WEIGHT: 330 pounds (150 kg)

DISCOVERED: 1902 by Lawrence Lambe

FOSSIL LOCATIONS: Southern Canada

Struthiomimus the
Ostrich Mimic

A lightly built theropod, *Struthiomimus* had a long neck, a small head with large eyes, slender arms, and powerful legs. It lacked sharp teeth or sickle claws for defense, so it relied entirely on its ability to sprint away from predators, at speeds as fast as 30 miles per hour (50 km/h). Its slender, toothless jaws indicate that it probably fed on large insects, small lizards, and possibly the eggs of other dinosaurs. Gastroliths, or gizzard stones, found inside *Struthiomimus* suggest it also ate plants and seeds. It had long hands with strongly hooked claws that may have helped it to dig out small animals or eggs, or to grasp leaves from high branches.

Grinding stones
Struthiomimus were toothless, but they did have smooth stones in their guts to grind up seeds and other hard plant material. Some modern birds also use this technique.

Size comparison
Struthiomimus was almost twice as high as a 10-year-old.

BUILT FOR SPEED

Like a modern ostrich, *Struthiomimus* had a body built for speed, with a long, stiff tail to counterbalance its weight, and powerful, long legs for fast running.

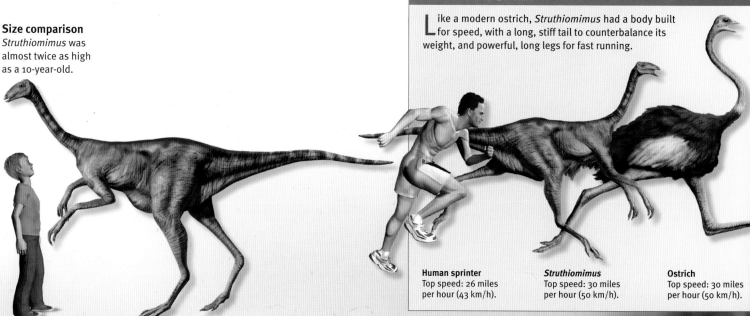

Human sprinter
Top speed: 26 miles per hour (43 km/h).

Struthiomimus
Top speed: 30 miles per hour (50 km/h).

Ostrich
Top speed: 30 miles per hour (50 km/h).

Opportunistic eater

Struthiomimus probably lived much like an ostrich today, using its speed to get away from predators. It had a widely varied diet that may have included small animals, insects, eggs, and some plant material.

Flexible neck *A long, flexible neck let* Struthiomimus *look backward, as well as forage into nooks and crannies.*

Naked skin *Its skin was probably similar to* Pelecanimimus, *which is known to have had smooth reptilian skin.*

Downy young *Most theropod young were covered in insulating feathery down.*

Hooklike claws *The long hands bore hooked claws for grasping plants or for digging up prey.*

Toothless smile *The jaws lacked teeth, suggesting that it could only eat small animals or crop plants with its beak.*

Prey Struthiomimus *ate whatever it could catch, perhaps grubbing out small mammals that lived in burrows.*

245 mya

TRIASSIC

208 mya

200 mya

JURASSIC

144 mya

CRETACEOUS

65 mya

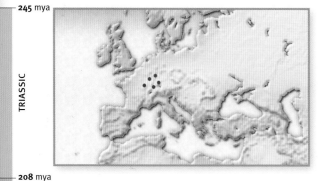

PLATEOSAURUS: THE FACTS

PRONUNCIATION:	Plat-ee-oh-saw-rus
MEANING:	Flat lizard
DATE:	Late Triassic
GROUP:	Prosauropods
DIET:	Plants
SIZE:	33 feet (10 m) long; 10 feet (3 m) high
WEIGHT:	4.4 tons (4 t)
DISCOVERED:	1837 by Hermann Von Meyer
FOSSIL LOCATIONS:	Germany, France, Switzerland

Plateosaurus the
Gentle Giant

One of the first large plant eaters, *Plateosaurus* lived in herds in Europe during the late Triassic period. It had a long neck, a small head with a robust body, and powerful back legs. It grasped plant material with its small arms, and chewed it up with its leaf-shaped, serrated teeth. *Plateosaurus* species varied in size from 16.4 feet (5 m) to 33 feet (10 m), depending on their local climates. *Plateosaurus* may have defended itself from attackers using a sharp thumb claw and large back claws. It is one of the first and best known Triassic dinosaurs. Many complete skeletons have been found in Germany.

Paddle-like pelvis
The flat, bladelike pelvic bones of *Plateosaurus* supported its large gut, built for digesting plants. The pelvis also supported the powerful tail and leg muscles.

Peglike tooth
Plateosaurus's leaf-shaped teeth had coarse serrations along the edges. It used these to cut the rough plant material it fed on.

Size comparison
Plateosaurus was just over twice the height of a 10-year-old, and six times as long.

Giant for its time
Plateosaurus may have been one of the largest Triassic dinosaurs, but it was dwarfed by the giant Jurassic sauropods.

Plateosaurus 33 feet (10 m); lived in Europe and Greenland, late Triassic.

Coelophysis 10 feet (3 m); lived in North America, late Triassic.

Eoraptor 3 feet (1 m); lived in Argentina, middle Triassic.

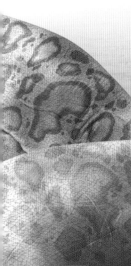

Life in the herd

Plateosaurus lived in large herds of 60–100 animals, and walked mainly on all fours. It occasionally rose up on its back legs to grasp at leaves in tall trees, or to defend itself against attackers.

Small head *Its small head had many leaf-shaped teeth for chewing hard leaves of conifers.*

Cheek pouches *Cheek pouches let it chew and process large mouthfuls of tough plant material.*

On all fours *Its tail was long and robust. This counterbalanced the animal's front when walking on all fours.*

Back legs *It walked on its strong back legs, rising up on its haunches to protect itself with its claws.*

Grasping arms *Small arms grasped at branches and leaves when it rested on its back legs.*

Thumb claws *These were sharp for defense.*

245 mya

TRIASSIC

208 mya

JURASSIC

150 mya

144 mya

CRETACEOUS

65 mya

DIPLODOCUS: THE FACTS

PRONUNCIATION: Dip-loh-doh-kus

MEANING: Double beam (after its vertebrae)

DATE: Late Jurassic

GROUP: Sauropods

DIET: Plants

SIZE: 88.5 feet (27 m) long; 16.5 feet (5 m) high

WEIGHT: 11–13 tons (10–12 t)

DISCOVERED: 1878 by Charles Marsh

FOSSIL LOCATIONS: USA (Wyoming, Colorado, Utah)

A lashing tail

Some scientists believe *Diplodocus* used its long tail to lash or thrash at its attackers. Lashing the tail made loud cracking noises that frightened attackers away.

Diplodocus and the
Cracking Whip

Diplodocus is one of the longest dinosaurs. Once thought to have walked dragging its tail along the ground, we now know by studying its skeleton that it held its tail aloft, supported by tendons. The long neck and tail were crested by short, broad spines. Its small mouth had peglike teeth only at the front, indicating that it stripped leaves off trees. Its enormous gut was supported by open ribs that enabled the stomach to expand when feeding. *Diplodocus* may have defended itself against attackers with its enlarged, sharp hand claws, and used its long neck and tail to strike attackers.

FLOATING SAUROPODS

One fossil trackway of *Diplodocus* shows only the front feet. This could be because the animal was floating in a river and putting its front feet down to stabilize itself.

Crocodile
Crocodiles float with only eyes and nose above water as they wait to ambush prey.

Diplodocus
When *Diplodocus* floated, its gut and tail were supported by water. It used its front legs to move.

Sonic boom
The thin tip of *Diplodocus*'s tail may have cracked like a whip, fast enough to create a sonic boom. This would have sounded like a cannon firing.

Chevron bones These small bones supported the tail's underside to protect blood vessels and nerves.

Size comparison
Diplodocus was as long as about 20 10-year-olds.

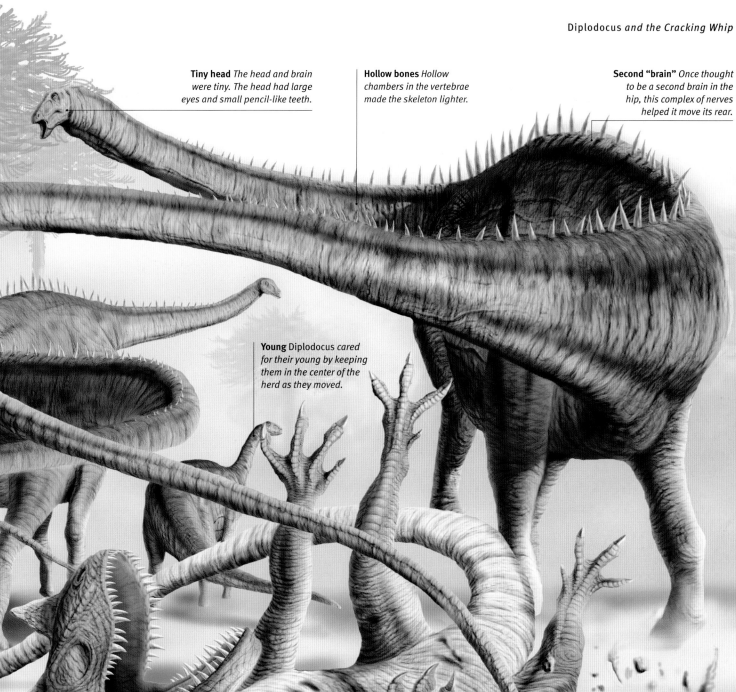

Tiny head *The head and brain were tiny. The head had large eyes and small pencil-like teeth.*

Hollow bones *Hollow chambers in the vertebrae made the skeleton lighter.*

Second "brain" *Once thought to be a second brain in the hip, this complex of nerves helped it move its rear.*

Young Diplodocus *cared for their young by keeping them in the center of the herd as they moved.*

Predators *Living alongside* Diplodocus *were several fierce predatory dinosaurs, such as* Ceratosaurus.

Whiplash
The end of the tail was thin, like the lash of a whip.

245 mya

TRIASSIC

208 mya

JURASSIC

150 mya

144 mya

CRETACEOUS

65 mya

STEGOSAURUS: THE FACTS

PRONUNCIATION:	Steg-oh-saw-russ
MEANING:	Roof lizard
DATE:	Late Jurassic
GROUP:	Ornithischians
DIET:	Plants, mostly ferns
SIZE:	39.4 feet (12 m) long; 13–16.5 feet (4–5 m) high
WEIGHT:	6 tons (5.5 t)
DISCOVERED:	1877 by Othniel Charles Marsh
FOSSIL LOCATIONS:	USA (Wyoming, Colorado, Utah)

Multipurpose plates

The back plates of *Stegosaurus* could have many purposes. It may have used its back plates to maintain its body temperature, to identify herd members, or to attract potential mates.

Stegosaurus and the
Bony Plates

Stegosaurus, a Jurassic giant, carried two rows of large, upright plates along its back. Its tail ended in four deadly spikes. It had one of the smallest of all dinosaur brains—the size of a small dog's brain. This was aided by a complex of nerves in its hip that regulated the animal's rear. *Stegosaurus* probably swung its tail from side to side, using its four almost horizontal tail spikes to defend itself from predators. The head of *Stegosaurus* had no front teeth but a beak for cropping plants. Fossils of its leaf-shaped teeth show little wear, suggesting that it swallowed ferns without chewing.

Bony core This supported the plates and anchored them to the spine.

Blood vessels Running across the plates, these helped to regulate temperature.

Temperature control *Large, sail-like plates were criss-crossed with blood vessels. Stegosaurus could have used these to warm or cool itself, by facing the broad side of the plates into sunshine or cool breezes.*

Skin Thin skin covering the plates may have been brightly colored.

Size comparison

A large *Stegosaurus* was about 10 times longer than a 10-year-old is tall.

Muscles Powerful muscles in the tail swung the heavy tail spikes.

Bone Robust vertebrae inside the tail supported the plates and spikes.

Identification *The plates varied between individuals. This suggests that they were useful in recognizing other members of the same species, or even different species, such as this* Tuojianosaurus *and* Kentrosaurus.

Spiky accessories
The tail had four large spikes, each 1.5–3 feet (0.5–0.9 m) in length, on its outer surface.

Protection *The back plates were large enough to make this* Kentrosaurus *look bigger, intimidating would-be attackers. However, they were too fragile to offer much real protection.*

Display *The plates had many blood vessels, suggesting that the skin around them could be flushed with blood. This could create intense, changing patterns to impress mates.*

245 mya

TRIASSIC

208 mya

JURASSIC

144 mya

CRETACEOUS

83 mya

65 mya

PARASAUROLOPHUS: THE FACTS

PRONUNCIATION:	Par-uh-saw-oh-loh-fuss
MEANING:	Side-ridged lizard (refers to ridged teeth)
DATE:	Late Cretaceous
GROUP:	Ornithopods
DIET:	Plants
SIZE:	34.4 feet (10.5 m) long; 13 feet (4 m) high
WEIGHT:	4.4 tons (4 t)
DISCOVERED:	1921 by Levi Sternberg
FOSSIL LOCATIONS:	USA (Montana, New Mexico) and Canada (Alberta)

Parasaurolophus and the
Strange Head

Parasaurolophus was a large, duck-billed dinosaur that sported a bony crest from the back of its skull. At first it was thought to be a snorkel-like breathing tube, but closer examination showed that it was a complex unit. Sealed at one end, the crest had hollow internal passages and connected with the nasal cavities. It was most likely a sound-producing system for creating loud noises. *Parasaurolophus* was a plant eater with many hundreds of small teeth, packed tightly together, and a horny beak to crop plant stems.

Head cases
Duck-billed dinosaurs often had unusual crests, ridges, or hollow tubes on top of their heads. These were probably for courting displays.

Saurolophus A short, pointed, bony ridge on its head may have supported a colorful flap of skin.

Corythosaurus A broad, semicircular crest on top of its head attracted mates.

Lambeosaurus An unusual crested ridge on its head had a short, backward spine.

Size comparison
The largest skull measures 4.5 feet (1.4 m), as long as a 10-year-old is tall.

TENDING THE NEST

Like other hadrosaurus, female *Parasaurolophus* fed their young until they were old enough to walk. This is similar to their relative, *Maiasaura*.

Resting It probably rested on all fours when feeding on ground plants or guarding the nest.

Juvenile The juvenile did not fully develop its crest until maturity.

Female The female's skull was the same size as the male's, but the crest was much smaller.

Sounding a warning

Parasaurolophus lived at a dangerous time when huge predators like *Tyrannosaurus* were at large. It probably lived in herds for protection, feeding on plants, and used its strange, bony crest to make warning calls when predators were near.

Airflow *Air flowed in from the mouth and nostrils through the passages of the crest.*

Nostril *This was above the mouth, not at the other end of the crest.*

Bone *Layers of bone divided up the cavity.*

Cavity *The cavity was a chamber for resonating air to make noise.*

Hollow crest *Parasaurolophus had a hollow, curved crest with several internal cavities divided off by layers of bone. The base of the tube opened into the nose and mouth.*

Warning call *By filling the crest cavity with high-pressure air, males may have produced a loud, trombone-like noise.*

Male form *The male probably had the longest crest to make the loudest noises.*

Raised up *It probably reared up to look out for approaching danger, or to feed from low branches of trees.*

245 mya

TRIASSIC

208 mya

JURASSIC

144 mya

CRETACEOUS

73 mya

65 mya

EUOPLOCEPHALUS: THE FACTS	
PRONUNCIATION:	You-op-loh-seff-ah-luss
MEANING:	Armed head
DATE:	Late Cretaceous
GROUP:	Ornithischians
DIET:	Plants
SIZE:	19.6 feet (6 m) long; 6.5 feet (2 m) high
WEIGHT:	2.4 tons (2.2 t)
DISCOVERED:	1902 by Lawrence Lambe; named in 1910
FOSSIL LOCATIONS:	USA (Montana) and Canada (Alberta)

Ankylosaurus Clubbed tail; last and largest of the ankylosaurs; North America, late Cretaceous.

Euoplocephalus and the
Lethal Tail

Euoplocephalus was built like an armored tank—bony plates and dangerous spikes on its back, shoulders, and sides of the head, as well as a double-headed solid club on its stiffened tail. Even its eyelids were protected by armor. Despite this, it was probably as agile as a modern rhinoceros. The one chink in its armor was its underbelly; attackers may have tried to flip *Euoplocephalus* on its back to get at its vulnerable stomach. Complex nasal passages indicate it had a keen sense of smell. Its weak teeth suggest *Euoplocephalus* probably ate a diet of fleshy plants and tubers. *Euoplocephalus* may have used its flexible legs and strong claws to dig for food.

Back shields *Shields on its back were made of thick plates and sharp spikes of bone. The largest of these were near the shoulders.*

Tail muscles *Powerful muscles, attached to a series of bones in the tail, supported the solid tail club's swinging.*

Size comparison
Euoplocephalus was slightly taller than a 10-year-old, and four times as long.

CLUBBED TAIL

The armored *Euoplocephalus* probably swung its tail club low and fast from side to side, aiming at the vulnerable legs and ankles of its attackers.

Club was covered in tough skin.

Muscles and tendons moved club sideways.

Long, thick vertebrae fused to the tail club.

Soft underbelly *The unarmored underbelly was its most vulnerable part.*

Armory of defenses

Armored ankylosaurs have been found on every continent, even Antarctica. Their success was due to using bony armor and clubbed tails for defense.

Minmi No tail club, but spikes on rear and tail, and with underbelly scutes; Australia, early Cretaceous.

Edmontonia No tail club, but covered in bony plates and spikes; North America, late Cretaceous.

Daspletosaurus *This large tyrannosaurid reached 40 feet (12 m) in length. It roamed North America in the late Cretaceous.*

Head horns *The horns protruding from the back of the head were short but very thick to protect the neck.*

Built for defense

Euoplocephalus probably lived in herds, sniffing out and digging for edible roots and tubers. Its spiked armor and clubbed tail were prime defense against predators, such as *Daspletosaurus*.

245 mya

TRIASSIC

208 mya

JURASSIC

144 mya

CRETACEOUS

71 mya

65 mya

PACHYCEPHALOSAURUS: THE FACTS	
PRONUNCIATION:	Pack-ee-kef-ah-loh-saw-rus
MEANING:	Thick-headed lizard
DATE:	Late Cretaceous
GROUP:	Ornithischians
DIET:	Plants
SIZE:	34.4 feet (10.5 m) long; 13 feet (4 m) high
WEIGHT:	4.4 tons (4 t)
DISCOVERED:	1940 by William Winkley (skull)
FOSSIL LOCATIONS:	USA (Montana, Wyoming, South Dakota)

JOUSTING ANATOMY

The domed skull was adapted to take head-on impacts and deflect the shock down to the spine. The skull's braincase was up to 10 inches (25 cm) thick, which left little space for the brain. The spine was strengthened by aligned vertebrae along its length.

Pachycephalosaurus and the
Butting Head

Pachycephalosaurus was known only from fragments until 1940, when a complete skull, almost 2 feet (60 cm) long, was found. It had a domed head of solid bone, with small spikes adorning the sides of the head and the snout. As with goats today, these were probably used for head-butting duels between males, or to fend off attacks from predators. The skull of *Pachycephalosaurus* was adapted to deflect the shock of head collisions from around the brain down to the spine. The spine bore thick ligaments that helped absorb the vibrations of head-butting. The teeth were broad and pointed, with ridges on the sides to help cut through leaves, seeds, and nuts.

Fighting for a mate

Pachycephalosaurus was a plant eater that may have behaved like modern goats and deer. Mating battles between males would have been fierce head-butting contests, resulting in loud cracking noises echoing through the landcape.

Heavy tail *The tail was held straight to align the spine, allowing it to absorb the impacts of head-butting.*

Size comparison
Upright, *Pachycephalosaurus* was about three times taller than a 10-year-old.

Guesswork As we have no remains other than skulls, these reconstructions are based on similar pachycephalosaurs, such as *Stegoceras*.

Long legs *The legs of* Pachycephalosaurus *were long. It needed the ability to build up speed for the head-butting charge.*

Bony nodules

Domed
head

Snout
spikes

Aligned
vertebrae

Small teeth

Delivering blow *The male
would have aimed his
attack to hit with the
center of his domed skull
for maximum impact.*

Receiving blow *If the blow
did not hit directly on the
head, but struck the body, it
could cause serious injury
to the receiving male.*

Female *Females probably
lacked bony adornments
around the skull. They may
also have been thinner.*

245 mya

TRIASSIC

208 mya

JURASSIC

144 mya

CRETACEOUS

67 mya

65 mya

TRICERATOPS: THE FACTS

PRONUNCIATION: Try-sar-rah-tops

MEANING: Three-horned face

DATE: Late Cretaceous

GROUP: Ornithischians

DIET: Plants

SIZE: 29.5 feet (9 m) long; 10 feet (3 m) high

WEIGHT: 6 tons (5.4 t)

DISCOVERED: 1888 by John Bell Hatcher

FOSSIL LOCATIONS: Western USA and Canada

Protecting the herd

Triceratops lived in large herds. Adults probably formed a protective ring around their young when danger threatened, as do modern rhinoceroses.

Triceratops and the
Three Horns

Triceratops was a rhinoceros-like dinosaur whose massive head sported a frill of solid bone and horns above the nose and eyes. This heavy and stolid animal moved flat-footed on all fours. It ate coarse plants with its horny beak and closely packed grinding teeth. *Triceratops* lived in large herds; abundant fossils suggest it was the most common dinosaur in North America in the late Cretaceous. Juvenile *Triceratops* had stubby horns that did not point forward until they matured. Fully grown, these horns were its main defense, but they were mainly used to ward off attackers rather than to charge at them.

Adolescent *They had well-developed horns above the eyes. These turned backward sharply. The frill may have been covered in scaly plates.*

Size comparison
Triceratops stood twice as high as a 10-year-old.

Young skull Frill is about 45 percent of skull length.

Adult skull A broad, pointed nose horn with large frill formed 70 percent of skull length.

FAMILY OF FRILLS

The horned dinosaurs (ceratopsians) had many frill and horn patterns, from single nose horns to spikes or holes along or in the frill.

Styracosaurus Large nose horn; six horns on the back of the frill

Centrosaurus Curved nose horn; two holes in frill with tiny drooping horns

On the attack Triceratops *would not have charged an attacking Daspletosaurus as its skull was too weak. Instead, it would have threatened the attacker with its horns.*

Adult *The horns of adult* Triceratops *pointed forward, and the nose horn was well developed. The frill was smooth with triangular tips along the edge.*

Juvenile *Juvenile* Triceratops *had horns that were starting to point forward. The frill developed a wavy margin.*

Baby *The horns of a baby were straight stubs above the eyes. It had a short nose horn and a boxlike frill with scalloped margins.*

Dinosaur Families

Dinosauria
All dinosaurs

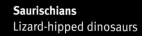

Saurischians
Lizard-hipped dinosaurs

Theropods
Meat eaters

Coelophysis
This 10-foot (3-m) agile predator with long arms and claws lived in large packs in North America.

Baryonyx
Huge hooked claws helped the crocodile-like, 29.5-foot (9-m) *Baryonyx* catch fish.

Oviraptor
This 10-foot (3-m)- long toothless eater of plants, seeds, and small creatures brooded its nest.

Troodon
A highly intelligent predator from North America, its large eyes suggest it hunted at night.

Guanlong
This ancestor of *Tyrannosaurus* was 6.5 feet (2 m) long and lived in China. A strange crest adorned its head.

Spinosaurus
At up to 59 feet (18 m) long, this was the largest of all theropods. It carried a high crest on its back.

Deinonychus
This North American "raptor" was 10 feet (3 m) long. It was a pack hunter with sickle claws.

Velociraptor
This 3.3-foot (1-m), sickle-clawed "raptor" was from Mongolia. It had a narrow wolflike snout.

Aves
Birds

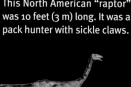

Struthiomimus

Allosaurus

Hesperornis
This early diving bird from North America lived at the same time as *Tyrannosaurus*. It caught fish.

Archaeopteryx

Tyrannosaurus

Ornithischians
Bird-hipped dinosaurs

Euoplocephalus

Ankylosaurus
This 32.8-foot (10-m)- long armored dinosaur had bony plates protecting its back and a defensive club tail.

Sauropods
Plant eaters

Pachycephalosaurus

Protoceratops
At 10 feet (3 m) long, this plant eater was one of the most common small dinosaurs from Mongolia.

Giraffatitan
This African plant-eating giant was 75.5 feet (23 m) long and towered 52.5 feet (16 m) high.

Diplodocus

Parasaurolophus

Maiasaura
This herd-dwelling plant eater lived in North America. It cared for its young in nesting colonies.

Barosaurus
A 85.3-foot (26-m)- long plant eater from North America, it had a narrow face and pencil-like front teeth.

Plateosaurus

Stegosaurus

Apatosaurus
This North American plant eater was once known as *Brontosaurus*. It had a brain the size of a modern cat's.

Melanosaurus
A 39.5-foot (12-m)- long African plant eater, it occasionally walked just on its back legs.

Triceratops

Iguanodon
This herd-dweller lived in Europe, North America, and Asia. It was the second animal called a dinosaur.

Glossary

angiosperm All flowering plants, such as grasses.

ankylosaurs A group of plant-eating dinosaurs such as *Euoplocephalus* that lived in North America, Asia, Europe, and Australia in the late Cretaceous. They were heavily armored with thick plates of bone, spikes, and bony nodules. They had thick skulls and clubs of solid bone on their tails.

articulated bones Bones that are arranged in their correct place in the skeleton.

bacteria Microscopic life that plays a major role in the decay of dead animals and plants.

braincase The part of a skull that surrounds and protects the brain. Dinosaur brains are rarely preserved, but paleontologists can work out the size of the brain by examining the braincase.

camouflage A way of disguising something so that it blends with, or remains hidden in, its environment. Some dinosaurs' skin may have been the same color as their environment to camouflage them from prey or other predators.

carnivore An animal or a plant that eats meat.

cartilage A soft, rubbery substance that most bone develops from as the skeleton matures. Cartilage is rarely fossilized.

cast An exact replica of a fossil bone or skeleton made in plastic, plaster, or resin. Soft tissue may also be preserved as fossil casts in stone.

Cenozoic era This began with the extinction of the dinosaurs 65 million years ago, and is known as the Age of Mammals.

cephalopod A group of soft-bodied animals related to snails that mostly enclose themselves inside hard shells. Cephalopods include squid, cuttlefish, and octopuses.

ceratopsians A group of four-legged plant eaters, such as *Triceratops*. Their large heads had horns and bony neck frills. They were one of the last groups of dinosaurs to evolve, and traveled in huge herds, browsing over the plains of North America and Asia for 20 million years.

cold-blooded Animals such as snakes and lizards are "cold-blooded." They get their body heat from the outside environment, by sitting in the sun. On a cold day they are less active.

conifer A tree with hard, needle-like leaves that holds its seed within cones. Pine trees are conifers.

coprolite A dropping that has become a fossil.

Cretaceous period The third and last geological period of the Mesozoic era, when many dinosaurs evolved and then became extinct. It lasted from 144 to 65 million years ago.

cycad A primitive, palmlike tree that flourished in the Triassic and Jurassic. Cycads had hard, woody stems with large, frondlike leaves, and reproduced by seeds in cones. Only a few species survive today, and all of them are poisonous to mammals.

erosion The wearing away of Earth's surface by rivers, rain, waves, glaciers, or winds.

evolution The changing of plants and animals into different species over millions of years. Dinosaurs evolved from their ancestors and then into different species during the Mesozoic era.

excavation Uncovering something and then digging it out of the ground. Any kind of fossil has to be excavated very carefully.

extinction The dying-out of a species or of large communities of animals and plants (called a mass extinction). Dinosaurs became extinct at the end of the Cretaceous. Their close relatives, birds, did not.

fossil The remains or traces of pre-existing life that has been buried and undergone a degree of change (fossilization). It may be the remains of a plant or animal that have turned to stone or have left their impression on rock.

gastroliths Stomach or gizzard stones. Some dinosaurs swallowed these stones to help digest food in their stomachs.

Gondwana The southern supercontinent formed when Pangaea split into two, a process that began about 208 million years ago.

hadrosaurs A group of duck-billed, plant-eating dinosaurs, such as *Parasaurolophus*. They had broad, ducklike beaks, batteries of grinding teeth, and many had bony head crests. They evolved in Asia during the early Cretaceous, before spreading to Europe and the Americas. They were the most common and varied ornithopods of the period.

herbivore An animal that eats only plants.

horsetail fern Primitive, swamp-living plants related to ferns. Horsetails once grew as large as modern tree ferns, but only a few small species survive today.

ichthyosaurs A group of fishlike marine reptiles that lived at the same time as the dinosaurs. They had dolphin-shaped bodies and gave birth to live young in the sea.

ilium The main bone of the pelvis. It supports the legs and is attached to the backbone.

ischium One of the bones of the pelvis. In dinosaurs, the ischium pointed downward and supported the muscles of the legs and tail.

Jurassic period The middle geological period of the Mesozoic era. It lasted from 208 to 144 million years ago. The conditions on Earth were just right for new kinds of dinosaurs to flourish, particularly the huge, long-necked sauropods.

Laurasia The northern supercontinent formed when Pangaea split into two.

mammals A group of backboned animals that have hair or fur and feed their young on milk. Humans are mammals, as are dogs, cats, and bats.

Mesozoic era The Age of Dinosaurs. It began 245 million years ago, before dinosaurs had evolved, and ended 65 million years ago with a mass extinction of plants and animals. It spanned the Triassic, Jurassic, and Cretaceous periods.

meteorite A mass of rock or metal that has fallen to Earth from a meteoroid in outer space.

mosasaurs An extinct group of marine lizards also known as sea dragons. They lived in inshore waters during the late Cretaceous. They had thick, eel-shaped bodies with four flippers.

mummified Dried out by heat or wind. Some dinosaurs were preserved in this way, after being buried in a sandstorm or volcanic ash. Even their skin and organs may have been fossilized.

omnivore An animal that eats both live prey and plant matter.

ornithischians "Bird-hipped" dinosaurs. In this group, the pubis pointed back and down, parallel to the ischium. All the ornithischian dinosaurs were plant eaters.

ornithopods "Bird-footed" ornithischian dinosaurs. This group included the hadrosaurs, pachycephalosaurs, and the horned, armored, and plated dinosaurs.

pachycephalosaurs The "boneheads," a group of plant-eating dinosaurs with skulls thickened into domes of bone. They included *Stegoceras* and *Pachycephalosaurus*. Most lived during the late Cretaceous period in North America and Asia.

paleontologist A scientist who studies ancient life, especially the fossils of plants and animals.

Paleozoic era The Age of Ancient Life, before the Mesozoic. It consists of six periods: Cambrian, Ordovician, Silurian, Devonian, Carboniferous, and Permian. It began 540 million years ago with an explosion of life in the Cambrian, and ended 245 million years ago with a devastating extinction event at the end of the Permian.

Pangaea The supercontinent linking all the modern continents. It formed in the Permian period and broke up during the Jurassic.

petrified Bone, or other organic matter, that has had its layers replaced by minerals.

plesiosaurs Large, fish-eating marine reptiles that flourished during the Jurassic and Cretaceous. Their long necks could rise above the sea's surface. They swam through the water using their four paddle-like flippers.

pliosaurs Marine reptiles, such as *Liopleurodon*, that had large heads with strong teeth, short necks, and sturdy, streamlined bodies. They were the killers of the Mesozoic seas.

predator An animal that hunts or preys on other animals for its food.

prey Animals that predators catch to eat.

prosauropods One of the earliest groups of dinosaurs, they were the ancestors of the long-necked sauropods. These plant eaters, such as *Plateosaurus*, lived from the late Triassic to the early Jurassic.

pterosaurs Flying reptiles, only distantly related to dinosaurs. Pterosaurs evolved during the late Triassic period, and had wingspans ranging from 1.5 feet (45 cm) to 39 feet (12 m).

pubis One of the lower bones of the pelvis. In saurischian dinosaurs, it pointed forward; in ornithischians, it lay parallel to the ischium and pointed backward.

reptiles A group of backboned animals. They have scaly skin, and their young hatch out of eggs. Snakes and lizards are modern reptiles.

saurischians "Lizard-hipped" dinosaurs, with the pubis pointed toward the head of the pelvis. Two-legged, meat-eating theropods and four-legged, plant-eating sauropods were both saurischians.

sauropods The four-legged dinosaurs, such as *Diplodocus*, with very long necks and tails. They had lizard-like hips, while most plant eaters had birdlike hips. Evolving in the late Triassic, they included the largest animals ever to walk on Earth.

scavenger A meat-eating animal that feeds on dead animals or carcasses. It either waits until the hunter has eaten its fill, or it steals the dead animal from the hunter.

serrated teeth Teeth that have sawlike edges. Many theropods had serrated teeth to tear through flesh.

species A group of animals or plants that can breed with each other and produce young that can also breed. A group of similar species forms a genus. *Tyrannosaurus rex* was a species of the *Tyrannosaurus* genus of dinosaurs.

stegosaurs Four-legged, plant-eating dinosaurs with bony plates along their backs, and long, sharp spikes on their strong tails. From the late Jurassic period, they roamed North America, Europe, Asia, and Africa, and included *Stegosaurus*.

theropods All the meat-eating dinosaurs. They were lizard-hipped and walked on their back legs.

trackways A series of footprints left by an animal walking or running over soft ground. Sometimes, dinosaur trackways became fossilized.

Triassic period The first geological period in the Mesozoic era, from 245 to 208 million years ago. Dinosaurs appeared about halfway through this period, around 228 million years ago.

trilobite Small beetle-like creature with three body parts that lived in the seas of the Paleozoic era. Trilobites became extinct at the end of the Permian, just before the Age of Dinosaurs.

tyrannosaurs A group of theropod dinosaurs with very short arms related to *Tyrannosaurus*, such as *Albertosaurus*.

vertebrae The bones along the spine, from the base of the skull to the tail. They protect the spinal column.

warm-blooded Animals such as mammals and birds are "warm-blooded." Their body temperature stays about the same, because they generate heat inside their bodies from the food they eat. They can be active all the time.

Index

Credits

The publisher thanks Alexandra Cooper for her contribution, and Puddingburn for the index.

ILLUSTRATIONS
Front cover Christer Eriksson (main), Karen Carr© (supports); **back cover** Leonello Calvetti, The Art Agency/Barry Croucher, Peter Bull Art Studio.
Paul Bachem 28; **Alistair Barnard** 11; **The Art Agency/Robin Bouttell** 10; **Leonello Calvetti** 4, 8–9, 11, 28, 32–3, 34–5, 60, 61; **Karen Carr©** 4, 6–7, 10, 11, 20–1, 22–3, 24–5, 26–7, 60, 61; **Brian Choo** 8, 32; **The Art Agency/Barry Croucher** 5, 10, 11, 38–9, 46–7, 50–1, 52–3, 61, 62; **Mark A. Garlick** 4, 18; **Steven Hobbs** 11, 28, 38, 40, 42, 44, 46, 48, 50, 52, 54, 56, 58; **The Art Agency/Steve Kirk** 28, 61; **Dr. David Kirshner** 60; **James McKinnon** 1, 3, 4, 5, 11, 12–13, 14–15, 16–17, 29, 40–1, 42–3, 44–5, 48–9, 56–7, 60, 61, 62; **Moonrunner Design** 60; **Peter Bull Art Studio** 28, 29, 30; **PixelShack** 28, 29, 36–7, 54–5, 58–9, 60, 61; **The Art Agency/Luis Rey** 60

MAPS
Andrew Davies and Map Illustrations

PHOTOGRAPHS
Key t=top; l=left; r=right; tl=top left; tcl=top center left; tc=top center; tcr=top center right; tr=top right; cl=center left; c=center; cr=center right; b=bottom; bl=bottom left; bcl=bottom center left; bc=bottom center; bcr=bottom center right; br=bottom right

APL/CBT=Australian Picture Library/Corbis; APL/MP=Australian Picture Library/Minden Pictures; GI=Getty Images; NHM=Natural History Museum, London; PL=photolibrary.com

11b PL **19**tr APL/MP **20**bl PL; br John Long **25**br NHM **26**bl APL/CBT **28**l Stuart Bowey; tc, tr PL **30**br John Long **31**br GI **32**tc PL **35**bcr APL/CBT; br GI **40**cl APL/CBT